HORSE
SOLUTIONS

25 EXPERT ANSWERS
to common horse problems

PUBLISHED BY
D J Murphy (Publishers) Ltd

A
HORSE & RIDER
Magazine Handbook

SPONSORED BY

Nutritional products for problems

If there is one thing that's certain about horses it is that life with them is far from boring! They test us in a variety of ways, whether they are being handled, ridden or when they are not well. HORSE&RIDER magazine receives countless letters from readers seeking advice and reassurance and, although there is not always one simple solution, our panel of experts is renowned for giving sensible answers to what can seem insurmountable problems. Horse Solutions brings you some of the more often-asked questions we receive at HORSE&RIDER magazine - and our experts' suggestions. At the end of the day, most problems can be solved - with a little help!

Kate Austin

First published in Great Britain in 2000
© **D J Murphy (Publishers) Ltd**

Editor: **Kate Austin**
Designer: **Jamie Powell**

Published by D J Murphy (Publishers) Ltd, Haslemere House, Lower Street, Haslemere, Surrey GU27 2PE. Sponsored by Natural Animal Feeds.

ISBN 0-9513707-3-1

Origination by **PPG Ltd**, Hilsea, Portsmouth.
Printed by **E T Heron**, The Bentall Complex, Colchester Road, Heybridge, Maldon, Essex CM9 4NW.

Acknowledgements: Many thanks to **Fliss Gillott, Rob Pilsworth, Kelly Marks, Jane van Lennep, Dr Marthe Kiley-Worthington** and **Dr Natalie Waran** for their answers to HORSE&RIDER readers' problems. Thanks also to Natural Animal Feeds for sponsoring *Horse Solutions* and to their nutritionist, Kate Jones, for her nutritional input.

Photos: *thanks to all the models who kindly posed for the photos published in* Horse Solutions. *Please note that, in most cases, the horses and riders shown do not have the problem they are illustrating but have fine-tuned their acting skills for the photographer! No connection should be made between the horse pictured and the relevant problem.*

THE AUTHORS

Dr Natalie Waran is a lecturer in animal behaviour and welfare at the University of Edinburgh and is also the Director of the postgraduate Masters course in behaviour and welfare. Her main interest is horse behaviour and she writes for scientific and consumer journals. She lives in Scotland with her family and various animals, including three Thoroughbred horses, and is a keen amateur competitor - when time allows!

Fliss Gillott BHSII, BHSI (SM), NPSD started riding at the age of two and was brought up with horses which completely took over her family's farm. Fliss went through Pony Club and Riding club activities and developed a lasting passion for dressage. She still teaches riding for a living and is reading Psychology with the Open University.

Jane van Lennep MSc, NPSD, BHS SM (Fliss Gillott's sister) also started out on the family farm/riding school. After qualifying, Jane ran a training stud/livery yard for 21 years and now breeds and competes with Endurance Arabs. Jane's approach to horse management is an holistic one, and constantly refers to nature and natural methods. Jane has written two books and she and Fliss have answered readers' equine problems in HORSE&RIDER magazine since 1983.

Rob Pilsworth MA, VetMB, CertVR, BSc, MRCVS qualified from Cambridge University School of Veterinary Medicine in 1981. He spent five years in mixed practice before joining Rossdale & Partners, in Newmarket, in 1986. He became a partner in the practice two years later. He has particular interests in diagnostic imaging and lameness diagnosis.

Dr Marthe Kiley-Worthington is a cognitive ethologist (studies the minds of animals) and an applied ethologist (applies scientific knowlege concerning animal behaviour to their welfare). She works with many species as well as horses and has written two books on horse behaviour and welfare. She runs a consultancy on behavioural problems and gives workshops and demonstrations nationally and internationally. Her own experimental stud was founded in 1959 and produces top performing horses.

Kelly Marks has been around horses her whole life. A successful junior show jumper and lady jockey, she retired from race riding in 1995. By this time, she had met, and started to work with, Monty Roberts who was so impressed he asked her to become the first teacher of his methods worldwide. Kelly is the popular equine behaviourist on BBC1's prime time programme Barking Mad, writes educational articles for HORSE&RIDER magazine, and gives a 'free lesson' each month on her web site: www.intelligenthorsemanship.co.uk

Kate Jones BSc (Hons) is a nutritionist for Natural Animal Feeds. After spending five years as an Applied Chemist, she gained a degree in Equine Science and started working for NAF. Her varied role involves liaising with vets, working alongside NAF's veterinary director, formulating new products, training retailers and giving lectures on nutrition. Kate can be contacted via the NAF Freephone Advice Line: 0800 373 106 or the NAF website: www.nutri.org

CONTENTS

Can you advise on how to get my mare over her fear of water? She is three years old. I have tried all sorts of things but don't seem to be getting anywhere.

This is a surprisingly common problem, with few horses willingly getting their feet wet without a very good reason. To them, there is probably little sense in wading into the unknown - how can they be sure it is not either extremely deep or dangerously boggy? It is certainly cold and wet. If you look at it from the horse's point of view it makes it easier to understand your filly's reluctance to take the plunge.

Associate water with positive thoughts and your horse may even enjoy it.

Working through fear

It is important that you work on her obedience and trust in you as a leader. This level of obedience usually starts to build as a horse learns to work either on the lunge or under saddle.

Going forward to voice or leg, not turning away from strange sights and sounds, but learning to work through these fears, and discovering that being obedient does not lead to harm but is a safe option - these things will be of great benefit. I would even go so far as to avoid water altogether until you have a greater rapport with her in other situations. Continuing to make an issue of going through water will only lead to her learning to be stubborn.

When the time is right, try to find a situation which involves crossing water, even if it is only a trickle across her path, because there is no alternative. This could be on the way home from a hack, or out to her field, wherever, as long as she feels it is worth getting to the other side. If there is a possiblity of going round the water, she will want to take it, in which case you may have a battle on your hands. This needs to be avoided.

Have an older horse there to give her a lead and be prepared to lead her yourself. With no fighting or hitting, be patient and wait for her to decide that she will have to go, even if it takes all day. Reward her as soon as she does it - she will be able to work out that you were right in saying it was safe and that it would have been easier to listen to you in the first place.

The only way you can speed things up a bit is by not letting her

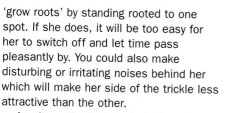

'grow roots' by standing rooted to one spot. If she does, it will be too easy for her to switch off and let time pass pleasantly by. You could also make disturbing or irritating noises behind her which will make her side of the trickle less attractive than the other.

An alternative to this method is to take her somewhere so sloshy that she has to get her feet wet; If it proves to be a wet winter, this should not be a problem. However, this is not always an option with a three-year-old, as going out for a sufficiently long and energetic hack to encourage her to drop her inhibitions and splash away could well be too much for her young legs.

A lot depends on the type of soil you have in your area, as wet clay exerts such a pull that this is likely to be off-putting rather than encouraging. The advantage of this method is that it is again making the object of getting wet less of an issue in itself and more a part of just being a riding horse and having fun. Riding out in a gang will help as part of this exercise. If your horse is out with bold and uninhibited others, she will be less likely to fuss about water round her feet and more concerned with staying with her friends.

Whichever method you use to get her started, the main points to bear in mind are that you are as non-confrontational as possible, that she is learning general obedience first, and that you move on in small, manageable stages which will not overface her.

Effectively, you are saying: We have to get from here to there, how will we do it? And she discovers that the only way just happens to be over water. It is best if she associates it with a positive thought in that she was brave and clever and you were terribly pleased with her.

Fliss Gillott

Is it too late to 'soften' my 12-year-old horse's 'dead' mouth?

He is sensible enough and doesn't run away or do anything frightening - he just seems to be totally insensitive to the bit. I have tried stronger and stronger bits, nosebands and gadgets, but he soon gets used to them and they lose their effectiveness.

It's always better to try to avoid problems in the first place, but I don't agree with 'it's never too late'. There may be hope here if you are willing to carry out some concentrated work with your horse.

It should go without saying that all necessary veterinary checks must have been carried out and, of course, in this case you would want the reassurance of knowing an expert horse dentist has examined his mouth thoroughly. At the same time, the dentist may have some comment to make about the shape of the horse's mouth or tongue which may suggest that one type of bit or another may be particularly suitable or unsuitable.

Some horses manage to suspend all feeling in the mouth - but you *can* rectify this.

Let us assume though that your horse is in good health, but to all intents and purposes he has managed to suspend all feeling in his mouth - how could we approach this? It would seem we need to think of another way of communicating our wishes.

Just say "whoa"!

I believe the way to go would be to try using a combination of voice and seat commands. The ideal environment would be an indoor school, but failing that, you need a high wall to ride at.

Walk him towards a high wall and just as he realises he has to stop, say "whoa" and brace your seat muscles. Let him stand for a few seconds and then ride a half circle of say 15 to 20 strides so you are head on to the wall and again ride straight at the wall. Just before he has to stop himself, don't pull on the reins, just say "whoa" and brace your seat muscles again.

Carry this out for a long enough period until you feel he's starting to get the message (learning times with horses can vary quite considerably, especially with the older horse). Then try the "whoa" and brace without the wall to help you. If he stops, give him a good stroke

and get off him right there. Let that be enough for the day. That will be a great reward for him and it will help the message to sink in.

Carry this out for several days until you feel confident enough to start similar work in trot. Once the trot is perfected, you can start work at a canter. Trust me - this method really does work.

Those of you who have seen Monty Roberts' *The Ultimate Horse Video* will have witnessed Monty's horse, Dually, perform the most incredible sliding stops from a full gallop - with no contact on the bridle at all - and later working in just a neckstrap! A great deal of Dually's training was carried out in just the manner described.

If you have enough patience and really work at getting your timing right and signals clear, you could get some real results. If he starts to rush his paces when you are riding, use the half-halt to re-establish control. If you work on using minimal contact with his mouth, you could start to regain some sensitivity.

If this was an experienced old show jumper or eventer we were dealing with that kept losing respect for any bit you use for any length of time, I would carry out the above procedure, but if I found a bit he went really well in, I would save it for 'special occasions only', for instance at a competition, and stick to using something milder for everyday work.

Kelly Marks

I've lost my nerve when cantering - what can I do?

The 15.3hh cob x TB gelding that I part own keeps running away with me in open spaces. I have tried changing his bit, and this works temporarily. I have had quite a long break from riding, and now find that, as a 34-year-old mother, I have lost so much confidence that the thought of asking my horse to canter makes me feel sick.

Galloping off in the way that this horse is galloping off is extremely dangerous. Many horses get a bit strong on occasions, but this is a world away from being totally out of control on a regular basis. Changing to ever-stronger bits is only ever going to be 'sticking plaster' and will only exacerbate the problem. Your horse needs schooling by somebody more experienced than you. He is quite likely to be no more than ignorant of the correct aids and therefore running away because he does not know what else to do. If the situation continues as it is, he could end up by being branded as a dangerous ride through no fault of his own.

It is not surprising that you feel nervous at this stage for the following reasons:

● The horse's behaviour is exceptional and you are justified in feeling frightened;

● Nearly everybody feels anxious after a long break. It takes time to rebuild riding muscles and to regain the feel you previously enjoyed;

● Being older, wiser and a parent changes your attitude to life generally. You have extra responsibilities; you feel that you may not bounce as well as you used to and that, until you are fully fit again, you are less athletic than you were. This stage will pass.

I would suggest that you do not ride this horse any more, or at least not until the problems are sorted out. Even if they are, I think you may find it difficult to trust him again, so perhaps you should consider having him schooled and then sold on.

I would also recommend that you allow yourself time to develop your riding ability and fitness on a quieter horse which you can trust, in an enclosed area. When it comes to cantering, concentrate just as much on the transitions in and out of canter as the canter itself. Then you will be able to rebuild your confidence in your own ability to control your horse. Enjoy the learning process without pressurising yourself into doing too much, too soon.

Tell yourself that you are capable of achieving whatever you wish to achieve. Being a mum is a reason to be cautious, but not to be negative or fall short of your potential. Knowing that you are physically and emotionally just as capable as you ever were is the first rung on the ladder to making serious progress. Taking up a challenge, learning and being active for yourself and not for other people, is a tremendous ego boost. Good luck with your riding!

Fliss Gillott

Lots of horses get strong on occasions - but this is very different from galloping off out of control.

Is there anything I can do to help my horse who has osteoarthritis?

About two years ago my horse was involved in a serious road accident which resulted, some time afterwards, in the formation of new bone on the knee joint. On my vet's advice, he was rested until the bone stopped growing. My vet said he would then operate to remove a loose chip of bone which was floating around in the joint.

Unfortunately, my horse is now much worse and completely unrideable. I love my horse dearly and do not want to have to put him down but I am worried that he may be suffering pain.

The accident your horse suffered sounds quite serious, even if it may not have appeared so at the time, and seems to have resulted in a 'chip fracture' of the joint margins of the knee. Unfortunately, once these 'knee chips' are present in a joint, they tend to promote the development of degenerative joint disease (osteoarthritis) in the joint, and this is an irreversible process. Most of the treatment we carry out on the joints in horses is aimed at controlling the progression of this degenerative joint disease and limiting its symptoms.

Once your horse is ready to do some work, start very slowly.

A progressive disease

We have to face the fact from the outset that osteoarthritis is incurable. If arthritis was a curable disease in man, for instance, nobody would ever need hip or knee replacements. These operations are carried out as a salvage procedure when osteoarthritis progresses to the same degree as you describe in your horse, and a person is in permanent and incurable pain. In these procedures the arthritic joint is removed surgically and replaced with a plastic prosthesis, but, unfortunately, this is not yet possible in the horse.

It is unlikely that the progression in the lameness is directly related to the surgery. The surgery was aimed at removing free floating 'chips' and, unfortunately, the progressive nature of arthritis means that these arthritic joints do become more and more painful with time, even after making an initial recovery from the traumatic incident, just as you have described.

Pain relief

Only you can judge the degree of pain your horse is suffering. If the horse is eating well and maintaining bodily condition, he is unlikely to be in severe and constant pain, as this usually causes horses to lose condition. It may be that your horse would benefit from being confined to the stable for a two month period to allow the joint movement to be limited and some degree of 'ankylosis' (or stiffening) to take place. This would result in a very stiff knee joint, but it may well be a less painful one.

Nature is a wonderful healer, and you may be surprised what a couple of months' complete confinement to the stable will achieve. In my hands this would be combined with oral medication with Phenylbutazone to limit the inflammation and the pain the horse is suffering. I would then get him out of the box at the end of two months, and jog him up and see what degree of lameness is present.

At that stage, I think you would have to decide whether you had to face the sad fact that this horse's useful career is over, or, if he was moving better than expected, then you could gradually introduce walking exercise, building to walking and trotting in the hope that he could retain some use as a pleasure horse.
Rob Pilsworth

Nutritional solutions

Although osteoarthritis is progressive and ultimately incurable, given the correct nutrients the body can support the joint, especially where the horse is fit and well in all other respects. Chondroprotective agents are universally recognised as being important to arthritis, both in animal and human medicine - they literally feed the joint tissue like for like. For horses it is believed glucosamine is of most use, although many animals get the best results from a combination of that and chondroitin sulphate.

Nutrients such as MSM or Devil's Claw are also useful where pain and inflammation are seen, especially when considering long-term, chronic cases.
Kate Jones

What is the best way to treat COPD?

My mare developed a cough last year which was treated with antibiotics. Her cough has recurred twice since then and it looks as though she has COPD. How can I prevent further attacks?

Soak hay for one minute before feeding.

COPD is probably the commonest cause of chronic coughing in the horse. It is caused by a hypersensitivity in the lining of the lung air tubes to fungal spores and dust. Its most similar equivalent condition in man is asthma.

It is not uncommon for a horse which has never previously coughed, suddenly to become sensitised to stable dusts, and this often seems to follow a primary viral infection. This may well be what happened in your own horse's case, and her first episode of respiratory disease and coughing could well have been due to infection.

In some horses it seems that once the respiratory tract has become sensitised, it remains sensitised for a period of time, sometimes the remainder of the horse's life. To be sure that your horse is suffering from COPD, we would probably need to have more information about the horse.

Firstly, does the cough disappear when the horse is turned out in the summer? Most horses with COPD improve considerably when not exposed to a dusty stable environment. Secondly, does your horse improve clinically, and does the cough rate reduce, when medicated with clenbuterol (Ventipulmin) only? This is a fairly sensitive indicator that broncho-spasm and mucus accumulation are the cause of your horse's cough, in that clenbuterol only acts by relaxing the airways and is not aimed at infection or other causes of coughing.

If the answer to both of these is positive, then it is likely that your horse is suffering from COPD. Once you have established this for sure, then you can go on to design a programme to minimise your horse's exposure to the allergens which cause the problem.

Managing COPD

Your horse should be bedded on newspaper or shavings and these should be kept clean and not allowed to rot in the stable. The hay should be fully immersed in water for one minute prior to feeding. Longer immersion than this 'leaches' a lot of the goodness out of the hay and is not to be recommended. All hay should be fed on the floor, so that the horse is not standing at a haynet pulling clouds of dust particles into the air which he subsequently breathes in.

Your stable should be well ventilated at all times. If this means leaving the top door open and having a window at the back, then so be it. If you are worried about the cold, you can always put more rugs on the horse, and standing bandages on all four legs to keep your horse warm enough. Remember that horses were designed to live in fields and were never designed to cope with the air quality which results from putting them in buildings.

Treating the symptoms

If you do all of the above and your horse is still plagued with COPD symptoms, then you could consider medicating your horse with a drug designed to prevent the allergic response from taking place.

Unlike Ventipulmin, these drugs are not designed to relieve the symptoms of COPD, but to block the cause. One such drug is sodium cromoglycate. This used to be available as a drug called Cromovet which was administered as an aerosol by a face mask. Unfortunately, along with many other medications, this has now lost its product licence. However, it is legal for your vet to prescribe the nearest licensed human equivalent and, fortunately, there is such a preparation made primarily for use in treating hay fever in man as an eyedrop.

This can be administered by nebuliser in exactly the same way as Cromovet used to be. The drug company concerned, Shearing Plough, would be happy to advise on the use of this product if your vet were to contact them. The administration of this fine aerosol is deposited on the lining of the airways of the lung and prevents a cellular reaction happening when the horse breathes in fungal spores and dusts. The mast cells, which are the cells which often deal with allergy and inflammatory response, are effectively locked away and unable to respond by the use of this medication.

In this way, although you do not prevent your horse inhaling dust, you do put a stop to the abnormal allergic reaction which is triggering your horse's symptoms.

Rob Pilsworth

Nutritional solutions

Nutraceuticals are useful in respiratory conditions. Herbs such as Anisum and Capsicum are used as expectorants and to promote the mucocillary response. In a recent trial at Cambridge University Vet School, garlic was found to actively inhibit respiratory bacteria. In severe cases a combination of garlic and naturally sourced antioxidants are of most benefit. Fruits are rich in antioxidants and this explains why it's a good idea to drink lots of orange juice and hot lemon when we have a cold.
Kate Jones

How can I ride my horse in a straight line? In dressage tests, we enter at C and wiggle down the centre line. Any suggestions?

Horses do not naturally move in straight lines. You only have to look at the tracks made by horses on old pasture to see this. A tendency to meander at slow speed is part of the horse's genetic make up. On the other hand, a fast-moving horse takes a much straighter line as this will give him the quickest route to his destination or out of danger.

With this knowledge, it is easy to see why impulsion is necessary to produce a straight line from the ridden horse. The two words 'forward' and 'straight' are so intertwined that you cannot truly have one without the other. Bear in mind that 'impulsion' is a desire to move forward, and not speed, although speed may be incorporated in impulsion.

Born one-sided

People are no more straight than horses. We are all, with few exceptions, born either right or left-handed and this affects our ability to ride straight. There is plenty that can be done off the horse to remedy the situation and to build the strength in the weaker side.

Remember to groom equally with left and right hands, to swap the yard broom from side to side, or to lift bales of hay using either knee to get the lift into the wheelbarrow - all these things will ultimately be of help in getting your horse straight once you are in the saddle.

Even if you are obliged to spend your day sitting at a desk in front of a computer you can make an effort to sit equally on your seat bones, and to have a straight back rather than flopping to one side or another with your legs crossed under the desk.

If you are having difficulty riding a straight line, the first step is to think forward and straight. Target a point in the distance which is beyond where you want to make your next turn. Each time you make a turn, find a new target. Ride in that direction with enthusiasm which will then be transmitted to your horse. The advantage of having a target beyond the corner is that you avoid a collapse before the corner - mentally you have never quite arrived, and so you are less likely to be tempted to stop riding forward.

Finally, imagine tram lines and that you are riding between the two lines. Your left leg and hand contain the left side, and your right leg and hand contain the right side.

Impulsion is necessary to produce a straight line from the ridden horse.

Using the correct aids

The way you use your weight and apply the aids is what, in the end, results in the horse being straight or otherwise. The more responsive the horse is to the aids the straighter he is likely to be. When you increase the pressure with your leg, he should respond, and when you close your fingers on the reins he should respond to that too. When this is the case, as long as you ride every stride forward, and clearly direct each stride, you will have a straight horse.

The more quickly you are able to respond to a change in your horse's balance, the less he will deviate from a straight line. In a fenced arena, the horse's tendency will be to collapse to the inside. Increased pressure from your inside leg, supported by a steady contact in the outside rein, will successfully keep the horse out.

Some practical exercises

Place pairs of cones in straight lines about 10m apart. It is much easier to hold a straight line over a short distance than a long one, so use your markers to work on riding a straight line over 20, 30 and eventually up to 40 to 60 metres.

Riding transitions on these straight lines will help to confirm straightness and will also give you much better transitions. If you are still having problems, try lengthening the stride to improve impulsion, working from one pair of cones to another before shortening again.

Include circle work before and after a straight line, with changes of direction to help you get the feel of riding forward from a turn.

Correcting crookedness

It must always be remembered that a horse will try to stay under the rider's weight. Unless you sit straight, your horse will always be crooked. We all need help from time to time with this one because

Horses do not naturally move in straight lines.

feeling straight does not necessarily equate to being straight. Your horse will try his best to tell you if you are crooked, but somebody on the ground will be able to tell you in what way you are crooked.

Using your weight to ride a turn, by shifting your weight in the required direction, will result in more subtle aids and leave you in a much better position to ride forward and straight from a turn.

An ability to ride straight will develop through constant vigilance. Just as a green horse needs teaching to work forward in a straight line before he does it instinctively, so does the rider. The more you work at it the easier it becomes!

Fliss Gillott

" How should I handle n new horse's aggressive behaviour?

She is getting more and more unpleasant towards me, especially when I groom her. She is a five-year-old 15.2hh, TB x Hanoverian. Her previous owner says that she was never 'touchy' before about being groomed. She seems to be resenting me more and more and has taken to 'darting' at me over the stable door. "

It seems that your young mare has learnt to be aggressive towards you. It is difficult to say why, but, as is often the case, she has learnt that by being aggressive things get better - in this case you leave her alone.

A common cause of this type of behaviour is over-zealous grooming with brushes that are too hard for that particular horse. The handler may just think the horse is being 'silly' and continue with the unpleasant stimulation until the horse finally finds that by biting and being aggressive, at least the person stops more quickly. If she has very sensitive skin, this may be the origin of the aggressiveness.

Keep her occupied

This is a young mare who is in need of more physical and intellectual work to do. Take her out for rides averaging at least 6mph (work it out and see what speed you do over, say, 10 miles). You can lunge and free school her and, as you do this, teach her to be obedient to your voice and body movements.

You should ensure that she has at least an hour's exercise a day, as well as time out in the field. Once you have got over the problem you can reduce it, but at the moment you do not want her to feel frustrated and bored so keep her physically and mentally busy.

If she is less aggressive with you outside, then tie her up in the field and, as you groom her, give her a tasty treat as a tit-bit like some cut up carrot, and talk to her as you gently groom her, scratching her on the withers with your fingers, and then rubbing your hands over her neck and shoulder and gently down her legs.

Encourage good behaviour

All the time she is not aggressive, tell her how good she is, talking to her quietly. If she starts making faces, just shake your head, frown and say no firmly. Then start again, using only your hand and fingers, with something she likes. Don't go near any place she has shown she really dislikes being touched at first, and build up her confidence that all you are going to do is give her pleasant sensations.

After a few days, you may be able to touch most of her body with your hand without any sign that she dislikes it. Then start with a very soft brush, and just go on quietly, but always be sensitive to her and if she is worried and aggressive, go back to a place she enjoys being touched. She has to learn to like you being near and that you give her a pleasant, not an unpleasant time.

Be positive

It is also very important that you are confident with what you are doing - any slight anxiety will reflect in your body language. She appears to cope with anxiety by aggression, and has learnt that it seems to reduce and remove the anxiety for her. Part of this may also be that she wants a strong reaction from you: she would like more of your attention and time to be able to develop a strong emotional bond. When you can groom her tied up, then try with her untied. If she moves away and apparently dislikes it, then return again to something she likes and work from there. Horses enjoy other things as well as food so find out what else she likes.

Remember, give plenty of praise if she does the right thing. If she bites you or is really unpleasant for no reason, smack her immediately. This is the way another horse would act towards her if she did not behave according to herd ethics and traditions. She needs to learn what she can and cannot do, and have it very clearly explained. She is still young and learning how to socialise with you as well as other horses and she needs guidance, so don't be too soft and never inconsistent.

Start from the beginning with your

mare and just try and enjoy each other's company and build on that. She is not trying to 'get away' with anything. She is after an easy life with friends, without strife of any type, so use your common sense and I am sure you will make it. She is obviously a very able and bright mare who learns very quickly, even to do the wrong things, and will be worth all the problems in the end.
Dr Marthe Kiley-Worthington

Nutritional solutions
There is possibly an hormonal element to this problem - becoming touchy and aggressive are the classic signs. Although her old owner didn't have this problem, there can be reasons as to why it has developed. Is she now kept with more mares? Are there colts or foals around? Perhaps the problem has developed with maturity? Try herbs specific for hormonal imbalance.
Kate Jones

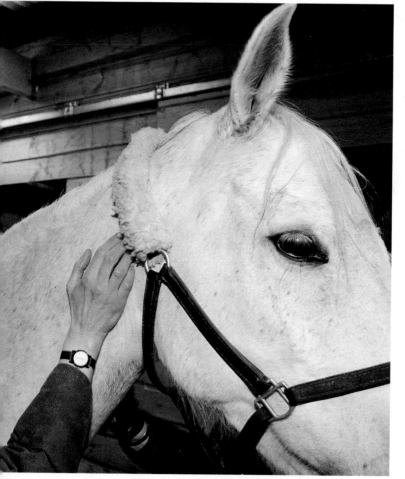

If over-zealous grooming has made your horse bad-tempered, go back to using your fingers and hands for a while.

How can I get my horse to stay quietly in his stable when I ride his stable companion out?

He rears, bucks, box-walks and sweats up. He can keep this up for two hours. He is fine turned out on his own, and he showed no such behaviour when on a prolonged period of box rest.

Your horse is responding in a perfectly natural way to a situation that, for him, is potentially life-threatening. The horse has evolved to live within a herd situation, where he is relatively protected from predation and other dangers due to the large number of individuals in the group. Their combined ability to spot dangers is better and they are able to confuse any predator by running as a herd. Most horses are, therefore, likely to be highly insecure if left in a stable when their companions leave the premises, unless they have been taught otherwise.

Your horse's response to the situation can be modified so that he learns that being alone is not likely to result in anything adverse happening to him. The problem is that up until now, he has reinforced his belief that being left alone is a frightening experience. By behaving in the way he does, the whole situation is made much worse, that is, he is frightening himself.

He has become caught in a cycle of behaviour that you must try to break. It's interesting that he does not show this response when placed in a field on his own, or when he was on enforced box rest. This suggests that his behavioural response is situation specific. He has learned that, in this particular situation, he behaves in a certain way, and that his behaviour is rewarded when his companion returns!

There are a number of ways you can try to change your horse's perception of the situation. Firstly, you must change the routine, so that he can learn the right sort of response in a new, related situation. I would suggest that he is placed in a different stable, perhaps his companion's, and that you change your riding time to coincide with his feed time, preferably in the evening after he has let off steam in the field all day.

Creating a distraction

You must find a way of occupying him whilst you get him used to being left for a short period of time. You will need the help of someone else who can keep watch over him, and reward him for good behaviour. I suggest that initially you use feed as a distractor, perhaps even getting him to work for his food, through using an Equiball.

Lead your other horse away from the stables when he is eating, and ask your helper to reward his good behaviour (being calm) with kind words, but ignore his bad behaviour by walking away from him. Return your other horse to the stables at a time when he is behaving well (which means that your sessions will have to be short initially). You can also try grooming as a good distractor, and, again, reward him for good behaviour.

Horses that don't like to be left alone need to learn that nothing bad will happen.

Gradually, as your horse's confidence increases, you can lengthen the sessions, decrease the helper's involvement and change the routine to suit you better. Your horse will learn that if he remains calm, that his companion will return, and that only good things will happen.

I would not consider sedation as an option, since all this will do is prevent him from learning a new response. This means that you will not solve his problem with being left home alone! In addition, it is apparent that just leaving him and hoping the problem will resolve itself (the 'he will get used to it eventually' approach) will not work for him because he has become overly sensitised to the situation.

However, if you are finding that you cannot break the cycle of his behavioural response to the situation, you should consider getting him a buddy (a small, elderly pony/donkey companion) who can help him to cope with his separation anxiety. Sometimes, the only answer to the problem is compromise!
Dr Natalie Waran

Is it OK for a horse with suspected colic to be allowed to roll? I have heard that you are meant to prevent them from rolling as it can make matters worse.

The myth that horses with colic should be prevented at all costs from rolling is one that has been established over the years. It probably arose because of the bowel displacements and gut twists that were found in horses which had been affected with colic for some hours and had been rolling. People put two and two together in the past and assumed that a twisted gut must have arisen as a result of the rolling. What almost certainly happened in these cases is that the gut displacement or torsion was the cause of the colic, and the colic caused the horse to roll, not the reverse.

A horse which is rolling violently in the stable can, of course, injure itself, and my advice would be to try and get the horse onto a soft surface like a sand school or woodchip arena if you are going to let it roll, to avoid the horse from injuring its head.

There is even some evidence that rolling may be beneficial in that certain types of large bowel displacement are now treated by anaesthetising the horse and rolling it from side to side in order to jiggle the bowel back into position. By doing this, it is now possible to avoid surgery on certain types of large bowel displacement; maybe this is why horses evolved the behaviour pattern of rolling in the face of pain to start with.

Similarly, horses with large bowel impactions, where they have massive distension of the colon with faecal material similar to constipation, will often lie still and hunch over so they are half way onto their backs. They lie in this position for long periods of time and, almost certainly, this relieves the weight of the impacted large bowel hanging from the supportive ligaments within the abdomen, and, therefore, takes away the dull ache associated with this condition.

Once colon impaction has been diagnosed I am certainly very happy for the horse to be left alone to lie still if they wish to do so.

Basically, colic in the horse divides into two types: those which get better on their own, and those that need surgical intervention. If there are no veterinary services available, and surgical intervention is out, then all you are really looking for is a period of pain relief to allow the horse time to establish whether it is going to be able to sort out the problem or not, and this is where the use of simple pain killing drugs, in the absence of any diagnosis, might be justifiable.

Rob Pilsworth

Rolling does not necessarily make a horse with colic worse.

How can I get my horse to stand still when I mount?

I bought him as a recently backed and gelded eight-year-old Arab, and he refuses to let me get on him. I cannot get him near a mounting block - he seems to panic! I have had his back, saddle and teeth checked and he has no problems. If I do manage to get on him, he then works happily.

Your horse is getting himself worked up into a state where he is showing little regard for his own safety, let alone yours. As long as this continues, the problem will not be resolved.

When a horse has been through as much as he has, it is not surprising that he is tense and unhappy. Until last year, he was full of the joys of his own existence as a stallion. Being gelded as a mature horse is a shock to the system, and he now needs time to recover. If the operation was followed quickly by being backed, he may associate the backing with a feeling of confusion. Being backed as a mature animal is as much of a change to a horse's life as being gelded. You now have the equivalent of a just backed three-year-old with hang-ups!

Teach your horse to stand still while you play around tightening the girth from the ground.

Step by step

Try breaking the process of mounting down into its component parts and sort them out one at a time.

The first step is to teach him to stand while you play around tightening the girth, adjusting your stirrups from the ground, and generally getting ready to mount up. Try to do this on your own, so that he learns to behave like a gentleman, because he wants to please you and not because he is forced to.

Be firm with your horse if he moves off, especially if he is pushy, and make much of him when he stands well. He should remain standing while you move around in front of him to get to the other side and back again. When he does this for the first time, return him to the box and reward him for being good. This may take five minutes, it may take several sessions, but it is important that he does it properly.

The next step is to take him to the mounting block without getting on. You may have to lead him past to begin with and halt close by. Make sure he is relaxed when he stands and respects your personal space. Again, do this on your own so that he is not intimidated and forced to fight.

Get him to the block in easy stages, taking as many sessions as are needed. You could perhaps lead him up to it for a small feed - sit on it yourself so that he is no longer tense when he is near it. Avoid even attempting to mount up until he is absolutely ready.

Even after all this, your horse may still try to disappear when you stand up on the mounting block. If you have managed to teach him, on your own, to stand by the block while you are on the ground, then you should be able to bring in a friend to help.

Your next step is to get him used to your being up a level, which could easily be done from a bucket or a portable mounting block. Your friend could hold his head while you do this, and offer him a reward when he stands. Give him lots of pats and words of encouragement from your heightened position, still without mounting up. Only when he is quite relaxed, standing with someone by his head, and with you up in the air on your block, even leaning across the saddle, will he be ready for you to slip into the saddle.

Breaking the cycle

It is vital that you break the chain of events that have led him to being in this state of panic. With time and patience on your side, and a willingness to learn on his, you will succeed. You need to be firm, but not bullying. It is possible that you will always have to take care getting into the saddle for the first time each day, but that is not a big price to pay. You may have to resort to being legged up while he walks forward until the problem is sorted out.
Fliss Gillott

Nutritional solutions

Nutritionally, the use of magnesium supplements can aid concentration without doping. These are often only required short term, as, once the horse has remained calm enough for the lesson to be learnt, it shouldn't be needed thereafter. Calming herbs such as Passiflora and St John's Wort may be useful.
Kate Jones

How can I 'wake up' my lazy horse?

He is a lovely-natured hunter type, but he is always very laid back when I am schooling him, to the point of being positively lazy! I feel as though I am the one doing all the hard work - is there anything I can do to improve this?

Before attempting to find a cure for this very common problem, it is important to work out the likely cause or causes. If the horse has always been lazy to the point of having been reluctant to lead as a youngster, he could be:

● Naturally lazy, in which case you will always have to work hard. However, there are always ways round this;

● Chronically malnourished (in the past if not now) or suffering from a long term nutritional deficiency. Blood screening may be useful in finding the right feeding routine, but in any case you should consult the vet if you suspect that this may be necessary. A genuinely lazy horse will become more determined to have his own way if you increase the feed, particularly the cereal content. A horse feeling under the weather will not respond to a change in diet;

● Suffering from liver damage, in which case he will need a specially formulated diet. You will need to talk to your vet.

● Of a genetic type which needs a serious incentive to make an effort! Some pony breeds, for example, can see no point in going round in endless circles, but will keep going all day if they are going somewhere - this is not laziness as such.

Physical causes

If your horse is not a type which is generally expected to be unwilling, such as TB, Arab, or any other similar 'hot' breed, or if he has been willing, and forward going in the past, but has suddenly become difficult, the causes may be quite different. For example:

1 Chronic or acute lameness, which affects both forelimbs and/or both hindlimbs, will not make the horse look lame necessarily. Look out for shortness of stride, going flatter than usual over jumps, or simply losing the spring in his step;

2 Hard ground not only causes concussion but also makes it difficult to grip the ground surface in turns, especially at speed. Talk to your farrier about this one;

3 Pain caused by an ill-fitting saddle;

4 Boredom and tiredness will cause reluctance to go forwards. Tiredness may come about through an imbalance of feed to work, too much work, or through a virus. The latter is very common during the show season, when large numbers of horses are being grouped together in one place;

5 Incorrect bitting, specifically overbitting, will discourage a horse from going freely forward. If you suspect there may be a problem in the mouth, ask a dentist to check his teeth. Pain in the mouth, from any cause, will have a similar effect;

6 Bad riding, whereby the rider is giving conflicting aids, albeit inadvertently.

Riding solutions

If your horse is still reluctant to go 'in front of the leg' after eliminating all possible causes, you must then look to your own riding for a solution. Few of us these days are willing to inflict pain on a horse to force him round to our way of thinking, which is as it should be.

Plenty of reward for good behaviour is the best possible encouragement, combined with the art of gentle persuasion, and simple logic. It must be nicer for him to answer the leg than it is not to answer the leg. If he does not answer, there needs to be an immediate reaction from the rider, which lets him know that you are not pleased. One way of doing this is to use your legs rapidly and hard on his sides, using them quietly and softly as soon as he responds. Combine this with a strong voice and command and he will soon get the message.

Artificial aids

Spurs

With a more experienced rider, spurs will provide a more precise and exact aid, which is better able to call the horse to attention than the more diffused pressure of the leg aid. However, without a rider possessing the ability to ride with a still leg, spurs may cause bruising.

Repeated over-use of the legs, with or without spurs, will lead to a deadening of the horse's sides. Constantly flapping legs cause resentment and less willingness to go forward.

Whips

A long schooling whip is almost essential with a lazy horse. Without inflicting punishment, it is possible to use it behind the leg with small, quick flicks, which will irritate - go on with this until a result has been effected. Swishing a whip alongside with a swinging arm is a useful aid, as long as you are confident riding one handed. All this will help to make the horse feel uncomfortable about ignoring the leg, and therefore provide him with an incentive to go forward.

The Wip Wop rope

Monty Roberts and Kelly Marks have found the Wip Wop rope to be invaluable for nappers. Used in a flicking motion just behind the rider's leg, it is very effective for forward movement.

The rider's seat

Last, but far from least, it is down to the rider to sit in such a way that allows, as well as encourages, the horse to answer the leg. Sitting tall and being able to follow the swing of the horse's back, rather than sitting stiffly in opposition to the movement, is the best encouragement of all.

With a sound, healthy, but lazy horse, you need to be balanced, coordinated, logical and imaginative. Keep your schooling sessions short, and finish on a positive note, and not because you are too exhausted to continue. Do plenty of hacking or jumping, for example, when conditions are suitable to keep your horse fit, and interested in his work. The lazy horse is just as challenging, in his way, as a fizzy one!

Fliss Gillott

The Wip Wop rope, an invaluable aid to encourage forward movement.

Nutritional solutions

Poor blood profiles most usually show up as anaemia which needs to be tackled with an iron supplement, preferably incorporating vitamin B complexes, copper and cobalt. Remember the importance of salt (electrolytes in hot weather or hard work) as lack of stamina is one of the first signs of dehydration.

Antioxidants are required if the laziness is as a result of physiological stress, either current or historical.

Kate Jones

How can I increase my 13.2hh pony's feed without making her too fizzy? She is kept out during the day and kept in at night and is fed horse and pony cubes as well as some bran. She is currently ridden every day.

You could carry on feeding the horse and pony cubes or a competition mix for more fizz. But take care - fizzed-up ponies can be pretty evil, so I'd advise increasing the cubes, and only switch to competition mix if she is seriously short on energy. Remember to make all changes of the diet gradual, taking at least a week to change from one food to another.

I do not recommend that you feed bran - it is deficient in calcium, which is an important mineral for all horses and ponies. Sugar beet pulp well soaked makes a better mash and can also be mixed with your cubes or mix.

There are lots of different feeds around and it may seem very confusing, but it need not be - once you have found a suitable cube or mix, stick with it because the manufacturer has spent a lot of time and money to make sure it is balanced and nutritious.

Good grazing and/or good hay has to be the basis of any horse or pony's diet and is so often under-rated. Fibrous food is not only what nature intended they should eat, it also helps to keep them content.

Should these cereal-based feeds, the cubes or a mix, give you too much of that unwanted fizz, try switching to forage cubes, such as alfalfa or grass. Alfalfa cubes are the least likely to fizz your pony, and can be used instead of horse and pony cubes or a lower energy mix. For more energy, but still less fizz than from cereals, try grass pellets. Using unmolassed sugar beet, which is increasingly widely available, will lower the fizz quotient even further. Fizz comes from soluble carbohydrates such as sugar and starch. Good quality forages provide their energy from fibre, which releases its energy slowly, without the fizz.

When exercising, make sure you don't put too much unnecessary strain on your pony's legs, so go easy!
Jane van Lennep

Nutritional solutions

Fat, in the form of oils (ie linseed oil) is an excellent way of providing non fizz energy. Horses adapt very well, but slowly, to oil as an energy source. Start off with a tablespoon and increase gradually over eight weeks.

Good doers are often micronutrient deficient as only a small amount of hard feed is given. A general purpose vitamin and mineral supplement is recommended for ensuring she has all the nutrients for health and vitality.
Kate Jones

Can I stop my young cob from throwing her head up and down when ridden?

It only happens in walk and particularly after trotting. She gets worse in the woods and then does it all the way home.

Head tossing is an increasingly common problem to which there is no single solution. Sometimes it appears to be a sensitivity to midges, a mild skin reaction or an irritation affecting the mucus membrane lining the nostrils. With these conditions, the problem is likely to be worse in the summer.

Generally, it makes little difference at what speed the horse is going, and may even be evident when jumping. In this case, the horse will be potentially dangerous to ride. The fact that your horse is worse in the woods suggests she may be reacting to midges which tend to like humid conditions.

Prevention

A fly veil covering her whole face will bring about an instant improvement if midges are the cause, or even an old stocking over her muzzle. As long as she can breathe through it, she will be unlikely to object, though you may find you are the butt of some very predictable jokes!

Head tossing may be caused by many factors.

It is possible that her head shaking has a different root altogether. Have you ever had your saddle checked for fit by an independent saddler?

Has your cob's level of work changed since you took her on? With a change in routine and diet, combined with the fact that she has only just reached maturity, she may well have changed shape, so the saddle which appeared to fit previously now no longer fits properly.

Either way, I would strongly advise you to get a Master Saddler over to check. It takes a trained eye to assess the pressure that is being exerted, particularly at the point of tree and the back of the saddle. When the horse is made comfortable, her behaviour may be very different.

Another possibility is that your mare needs her teeth rasped. Sharp edges can chafe the inside of the cheek or even the tongue long before the horse goes off its food, or displays difficulty in eating.

Get her back checked as well. A good cob rarely needs treating, but if her saddle has been ill-fitting or she has been poorly ridden at any time, then she will feel better for a massage.

All these checks will cost money, but once everything is as it should be, the expense will have been worth it. A twice yearly 'service' should keep things right!

Ride with quiet hands

As far as your own riding is concerned, you should look at the way you are sitting, as well as your hands and the contact you have on her mouth. When riding off the road on a well behaved horse, it is not necessary to have any contact at all. This does not mean you have your reins hanging in festoons, but rather that you have her on a long rein.

Nutritional solutions

Antioxidants are recommended for allergies, which are sparked off by a cascade of free radical toxins.
Kate Jones

Should you need to take a contact, in the event of her shying for instance, then you can quickly take up the reins. In the meantime, she will appreciate being left completely free.

Unless you are basically well balanced without reins, you will feel insecure. If this is the case, then you must work on putting things right. Any horse is likely to head toss if kept on a contact for an hour and a half, particularly with an unbalanced rider on board. Having good hands comes from having a good seat, which in turn is developed through training and practice. This is always important, even for quiet hacking on a well-behaved cob, and any horse appreciates sympathetic riding.

What happens if you ask her to go on the bit in walk? Done properly, this sometimes has the effect of steadying the head and improving the horse's balance. You say she is worse after trotting, so perhaps she is constantly expecting to go faster again and finds it difficult to settle. A few moments on the bit, followed by allowing her to stretch down towards the ground on a loose rein, may help to settle her back into walk.

If she continues to nod her head, even though she is unable to throw it up and down, this would suggest the problem is physical and she cannot help behaving as she does.
Fliss Gillott

Should I rest my recently backed gelding?

He's a three-year-old Welsh Cob x TB who is now hacking out quietly. He also has half an hour's schooling and a lunge lesson once a week. I am being given conflicting advice on what would be best for him.

There is no cut and dried solution to what is or is not right for a youngster as each horse is different. Physical maturity is only a part of the picture, as mental attitude and opportunity for natural exercise will also influence the needs of the individual. It goes without saying that too much work on young joints may lead to irreparable damage and thus shorten the horse's potential working life.

Training to suit the individual

A young horse will thrive on mental stimulation. It is naturally curious at this stage and therefore very receptive to new experiences. As he gets older he will be more set in his ways and take longer to learn the basics of being a mannerly and confident riding horse.

Some horses are still very suspicious and afraid of leaving their companions by the age of three, and will not benefit from doing too much at this age. Another year will see them grow in stature (mentally) so they become a much easier prospect to train.

Other young horses badly need to have some sort of discipline through light work, even as two-year-olds. These are the over-confident youngsters, generally big, strong and well grown, which may not have experienced the natural discipline of living amongst a number of older, and therefore higher ranking, horses.

From the mental point of view, a well mannered tractable young horse will suffer no ill effects from being given a holiday. A rest at this stage will give it a chance to mature physically so that it is better able to start work properly as a four-year-old.

From the description you give of your young horse, I would think that the work you have given him thus far has been ideal for allowing him a chance to see the world and understand what it means to be a riding horse. He obviously has some growing to do. While he is out of balance through having grown up behind, he will find it difficult to work correctly, and will be prone to minor back problems. Until he has levelled up, you would be better keeping him to light work only.

If you take a break from ridden work, use the time to develop a closer rapport with your young horse.

Monitor his progress

Look out for signs that your horse has had enough. Check his legs daily for heat, swelling and tenderness, especially around the joints. Take notice of his attitude towards you on work days. If he becomes grumpy or aggressive, difficult to tack up, reluctant to leave his stable when he is normally willing and cheerful, or displays any other changes in

personality, take note. He could be trying to tell you he cannot cope!
Also, take notice if he suddenly becomes lazier than usual, or clumsy,
goes off his food or loses weight for no apparent reason.

If you know your horse, and are observant, you will know when he
needs a break. Likewise, if you decide to lay him off and he shows
signs of being bored and depressed, perhaps he would benefit from
being brought back into light work earlier than you thought.

Give him a break

On balance, I come down on the side of resting young horses after
lightly working them as three-year-olds. The extra handling and training
invariably benefits them in some form, and they generally come back
the following spring with a more mature attitude and better able to
continue their schooling.

There is always a slight risk of being tempted to do too much, too
soon, in order to ring the changes if you keep horses going without a
break. In the end, you must make your own decision based on your
horse and your circumstances. Erring on the side of caution, however,
is more likely to result in being able to enjoy a long and happy
partnership with your horse.

Fliss Gillott

Most young horses
benefit from
having a rest - and
enjoy a little extra
handling and
grooming.

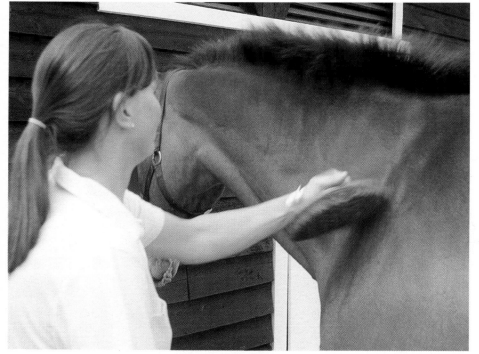

"Is it a good idea to lunge my horse?

I have heard that 20 minutes of lungeing is the equivalent of one hour of riding and I am wondering whether it is OK to lunge him two to three times a week. Do I need to invest in lots of specialist equipment?"

Lungeing is an art form, just as much as riding, and can be as strenuous or as gentle as the trainer wants it to be. Generally speaking, 20 minutes of unremitting trot work on the lunge will be just as energy-consuming as one hour's light ridden work.

It is advisable to use protective boots or bandages on all four limbs during lungeing. It is all too easy for the horse to strike into himself if he is tired, or shies, or if his action is not quite straight. Using side reins will help to keep him straight (that is with his hind feet following

the tracks of his front feet and not swinging wide) and to encourage him to work with a rounded outline. If the horse is obedient on the lunge it is much easier to keep him working in a good rhythm. A lungeing session divided between all three gaits may last for 40 minutes or more without the horse suffering from undue strain and can be done every day of the week, if necessary, but only if you really know what you are doing. Generally, 20 to 30 minutes is plenty.

Keep it interesting!

Lungeing need not be boring. Learn to move your circle around the schooling area. This gives you an opportunity to work in a straight line between circles so that you can check for straightness, improve balance, and start to work on varying the length of stride within gaits. Put in occasional transitions and teach your horse direct transitions, ie walk to canter.

If your horse is obedient and controllable in a headcollar, then there is no need to use a lunge cavesson. I prefer to lunge from the bit if a headcollar does not provide a safe level of control. Lungeing in a safe, enclosed area minimises the risk of the horse pulling away from you - a risk which is greater when lungeing from a headcollar.

Assess the work

Watch for the following indicators that your horse is working correctly:
- A runny, watery nose, followed by mouthing the bit;
- Reaching down with his head, towards the ground, and rounding and extending the whole of his topline;
- Stepping well under his body with his hindfeet, without swinging his quarters out;
- An even distribution of warm-to-the-touch, working muscles. An over-excited horse which is not working correctly will sweat up over the forehand before he sweats around his hindquarters.

Use these signs, as well as the clock, to decide when is the best time to stop. Make frequent short breaks to talk to your horse, make a bit of a fuss of him and change the rein. Take the side reins off from time to time to let him have a stretch.

Lungeing is a marvellous way to assess, observe and extend your horse's level of schooling. If you are prepared to put in the effort, you will reap many benefits.

Fliss Gillott

Keep your lungeing sessions interesting, with plenty of variety.

How can I prevent my horse from suffering another attack of laminitis?

She was ill with it two years ago, and I have since started a course of treatment with an holistic vet. She has fresh herbs and is turned out in a muzzle for a short time every day. At the moment she is sound and in work but dare I risk letting her have grass again?

The typical stance of a horse with laminitis.

L aminitis is an extremely common disease. The laminae are the 'glue' which holds the pedal bone to the horn of the hoof. A horse standing on its hooves is effectively hanging from the hoof wall on its laminae, just as if we were balancing on the tip of our finger nails. The laminae are therefore an extremely vital structure and any loss of viability in the laminae can result in quite severe lameness.

What causes laminitis?

Whilst we do not yet fully understand what causes laminitis in every case, we are now becoming increasingly aware that the primary event which triggers laminitis is a constriction of the blood vessels which supply blood to the laminae. This is usually the result of poisons, called endotoxins, found in the cell walls of bacteria, being released into the blood stream.

There are two common ways for this occur. Firstly, the horse can eat sufficient lush carbohydrate rich food that the bacterial balance in its intestine is thrown out of gear because of the rapid fermentation of the starch in the large bowel. Certain toxic bacteria begin to predominate; absorption of the toxins produced by them leads to the laminitis.

A second way laminitis can occur is for a horse to have an infection, for instance a brood mare with a retained placenta after foaling. In this case the toxins are produced directly by the infected area but nevertheless commonly result in the development of laminitis. The bacterial cell wall toxins are thought to trigger spasm in the blood vessel walls throughout the body.

This vasculitis is not really serious in many instances in the body and results only in symptoms like filled legs, but in the feet, because of the unique architecture of the blood vessels, the constriction of the blood vessel wall results in blood shunting around the short circuit loop which is present in the foot and returning to the heart without actually having entered the laminae.

It is thought that this 'shunting' has been put in position in nature to enable horses to stand on extremely cold ground, such as snow and ice, without constantly losing heat through the feet. The shunting system is therefore an advantage to the horse in the wild, but it becomes a disadvantage in the face of compromise to the blood vessels to the laminae.

Preventing further attacks

Once a horse has had severe laminitis, the laminae are often never quite the same and for this reason the horse is often prone to intermittent bouts of mild laminitis in the future. These can be controlled to some extent by sound management.

The only time that grass is really dangerous to your horse is usually in the spring when the first lush grass begins to grow and in the autumn when a long dry period through the summer is followed by rain and sunshine. What happens at these times of year is that the grass becomes extremely rich in easily digestible carbohydrate, and it is this carbohydrate which causes laminitis in horses and ponies. I think it would therefore be wise for you always to restrict your horse's grazing to a maximum of 15 minutes daily in spring and autumn when these rapid growing conditions occur.

During long, hot, dry summers, when the grass is yellowed off, you could probably safely allow your horse to graze for much longer, probably an hour morning and night would be safe. Similarly in the winter when the grass has very little food value in it, you would probably be able to allow your horse free access to grass.

Rob Pilsworth

Nutritional solutions

Research recognises free radical toxins to be the major players in both the cause and acceleration of laminitis. Therefore, antioxidant nutraceuticals are strongly recommended. Introduce prior to the risk period and feed alongside sound management.

Risks can be year round. Bouts are often seen following a hard frost, and although we are not clear on why this happens, 'loading up' with antioxidants is recommended then.

Fructans in grass are considered a trigger and are higher in the morning. Therefore, when limiting turnout try to keep it to a short period of the afternoon.

A broad spectrum vitamin and mineral supplement is essential for any animal on a severely restricted diet.

Kate Jones

Can you advise me on how stop my horse from hollowing? Every time I go from rising to sitting trot, he raises his head and hollows his back.

If your horse starts to hollow when you sit to the trot, you will need to address any problems you may have with your riding position.

In theory, it should make no difference to the horse whether the rider is in sitting or rising trot. The horse is the only thing keeping the entire weight of the rider off the ground, so that even when the rider stands up in the stirrups, some part of the horse's back is still bearing weight.

What does make a difference is the rider's ability, or otherwise, to sit still in the saddle. An unbalanced rider may thump down during rising trot, but is likely to cause even more discomfort by bumping around in sitting trot. A good rider is no hindrance to the horse at all in sitting trot, so if you have a horse which hollows when you sit, then you have a responsibility to learn to sit correctly. This is very much a rider problem rather than a horse problem!

Sit tall

Sitting correctly in the walk is much easier than sitting correctly in the trot, simply because there is less bounce. However, it is in the walk that you need to start perfecting your position. It is particularly important to sit tall, maintaining the natural slight hollow in your back without stiffness.

Only tense the muscles needed to maintain posture and balance as well as the forward movement of the horse. Keep your abdominal muscles stretched to counter any tendency to collapse and hunch up when the horse moves into trot.

The really crucial part of your anatomy is your seat. Allow the pelvis to absorb the movement of the walk whilst remaining upright, not tilting either forwards or backwards. In the walk, the horse's back has a lot of side to side movement, which you will feel increase as you accept the movement in your seat/pelvis/lower back area. Your seat bones should remain pressing gently but firmly straight down into the saddle.

Ask for trot when your horse is well prepared to trot, not from a lot of pushing and shoving on your part. It is much easier to ride well if you do not have to work too hard. Maintain the position you had in walk. It may help to tilt your pelvis very slightly back if your horse has a big trot so that you do not get 'left behind' or if you feel that you have a tendency to get 'bounced' up the back of the saddle.

Only trot a short distance and keep the trot quite slow and in a steady rhythm. It requires a lot of concentration to sit still and remain supple if you are in the habit of feeling uncomfortable. Short spells of concentration are easier to maintain; your confidence in your ability to sit properly in sitting trot will improve if you make sure of success.

Help your horse to help you

As far as the horse is concerned, it is easier to ride well on a well schooled and comfortable horse. So it is important to encourage your horse to work well at the same time as improving your seat. Make quite sure that your horse is working in a correct outline in walk, and that this outline is maintained through transitions.

Keep the trot slow so that you have a better chance of being able to sit still and therefore ride effectively, which in turn means you have the opportunity to keep the horse round in his outline.

Once you have been able to establish good results in short, slow trots, you feel a lot more confident about being able to keep everything together for longer spells. From here, start to increase impulsion, but always, always retaining the steady deep seat in the saddle absorbing, not resisting, the movement. Stretch your abdomen up and forward while your legs stay long down the horse's sides. Think positive!

Fliss Gillott

How can I calm down a nervous traveller?

My daughter's pony is very good in every way except that he is a terrible traveller. He loads into our lorry without any problem, but as soon as we put the partitions across he goes beserk.

O bviously the possibility of bad driving cannot be ignored. With the power of some of the cars that pull trailers nowadays, particularly once the state of the art stereo system is blasting out, it's no wonder that there are horses getting some hair raising journeys! So my first recommendation, whether you are driving a horsebox or a trailer, is TAKE IT STEADY and drive particularly carefully around bends.

Horses prefer to travel at an angle of 45 degrees. Many modern horseboxes are designed so that horses travel 'herringbone' style at this angle.

An instinctive response

There are several other things to understand in this case though. Firstly, horses balance so much better if they can spread their legs out when travelling. Secondly, it is crucial to understanding many aspects of horsemanship that horses are 'into pressure' animals - it is their natural inclination to push back into whatever is pushing into them.

The reason for this stems back to the days when horses had to try to survive attacks from wild dogs. Dogs would naturally go for the soft underbelly area and around the flanks and stifle. If they could get a little bite in there and hang on they could eventually pull out the horse's entrails. Although the horse would want to run away he would also try and push down on the dog to try and prevent it pulling out his insides.

If your pony can't balance he will lean into the partition and then press into it more and more because he believes it's going to eat him up. The horse will always lean into the turn. With the horse that fights the left turn, hip bone against the left and feet scrambling to the right, it's your left turn that really unsettles him. If the solid partition is on his left side and there is a solid wall on the right side, then when he leans over against the partition, the only place for his legs to go is up the wall, and that's where all the thrashing and fighting comes from.

You're better off travelling him with no partition at all than a solid partition. As the lorry goes round to the left he will lean to the left and his feet will go over to the right. You don't have to worry about him knocking against the horse next door, because his travelling companion's feet will come over to the right as well. The chances of them stepping on each other are virtually nil, though if you still feel anxious you can make sure they are well booted and/or bandaged-up - a wise precaution when travelling that should be done in any case.

Rebuilding his confidence

Now that this pony has been so badly traumatised you're going to need to start by travelling him on his own, loose, so that he can regain his confidence. If you could watch him you would see that when loose he will nearly always choose to travel at an angle of 45 degrees.

It's going to be necessary to take some regular, very steady journeys, and although he may flounder a little at the beginning of each journey while he remembers his old traumas, just keep going gently while he learns for himself that he is able to balance now.

If this pony could learn to travel happily loose, the next stage would be to give him a double stall. Ultimately, you could try him in a single stall positioned at a 45 degree angle. There must be room at the bottom of the partition, if you still feel it is necessary to have one, for him to spread out his legs.

If they are given the choice between travelling straight forwards or straight backwards, horses prefer to travel backwards. A recent report in the Veterinary Record showed that Thoroughbreds transported facing backwards had lower heart rates, neighed less often and maintained better balance. Their heart rates were also lower when loaded backwards. A backward facing horse can cope better with the swaying of the trailer, which is more pronounced at the back, and can also sit into the trailer when the driver brakes.

Safe travelling

The floor of the trailer needs to have a solid non-slip surface. Make sure there is plenty of air circulating around the trailer, though not cold drafts directly onto the horse's body or face. Horses really like as much natural light as possible and especially to see where they are going. Haynets can't cure bad travellers, but if a horse is willing to eat on his journey, it's at a least a sign he isn't too distressed. Anything that relaxes a horse is a good thing.

Kelly Marks

Nutritional solutions
See page 28 - the same applies to this problem.
Kate Jones

"What can I do to encourage my 16.3hh TB cross gelding to go out on hacks alone?

He will not walk out of the yard and runs backwards rearing, he barges into things and, despite my aids to move forwards, he can become quite dangerous. I have had his tack and back checked and he is fine in the school or hacking in company."

A very large number of horses object strongly to being hacked out alone. In many ways this is not really surprising since horses are herd animals. To be isolated is to be vulnerable. It is only through systematic training from an early age that any horse learns and accepts that it is safe when ridden out without the company of another horse.

As with many schooling problems, there are two ways of tackling the situation. One is through patience, firmness and logic, the other through force.

Hacking out alone goes against a horse's natural herd instinct. Horses need to learn that they are safe when hacking without company.

A forceful approach

The greatest ongoing difficulty with the use of force is that, without a strong rider on board, the horse which has been forced to perform against his will is going to revert to his old ways as soon as the opportunity arises. Unless a horse is confident and happy to do as he is asked, he is not going to continue to do it.

'Force' does not necessarily involve pain - a strong rider should be able to 'force' a horse to go forward without resorting to the use of whips and spurs, though there are very few riders who are capable of doing this.

Once a battle has started between horse and rider, the horse will remember the battle. Whenever he finds himself in a similar situation, he will once again remember the anger/pain/aggression and the situation is ultimately made worse. There are horses which appear to respond positively to the use of the whip, and there are occasions when its moderate and well-timed use is of benefit. However, a horse which is fighting against its misuse rapidly becomes potentially dangerous.

An alternative approach

This brings us back to the alternative methods, involving patience, firmness and logic. Knowing that a nappy horse is behaving normally is the first step towards successful retraining.

Unfortunately, you do not have any way of telling with this particular horse whether or not he has suffered from bullying in the past, so he may have all sorts of hangups to overcome as well as his instincts.

You still need to build up his confidence. Part of this comes from obedience, and knowing that being obedient results in a pleasant situation, whereby he is rewarded and not placed in any form of 'danger'.

While you cannot at the moment make him go forwards when he does not want to, nor prevent him from going backwards, you should have some control over where he goes. When he starts to back up, try to stay calm and ride as though this was exactly what you intended to do. Maintain a contact on his mouth, albeit light, sit still and keep your legs close to his sides. Leaning forwards, dropping the contact and flapping your legs wildly puts you in a very vulnerable position with little or no control over the horse.

If you are out of control, you are totally unable to restore the horse's willingness to work for you. So, as he backs, steer him either straight or round a turn. Let him know that, although you would prefer him to go forwards, you are not afraid or upset if he goes backwards or even if he stands still. If he stops completely, he will soon get bored and want to do something more active again. Eventually you will find he wants to go forwards again. When he does, praise him quietly with your voice and a pat on the side of his neck.

Taking him out in company will give you the best opportunity to teach him to go out on his own. Encourage him to take a lead, but if he balks, let the other horse come up alongside him. Gradually increase the distance between the two horses and, if possible, take separate routes for the last stretch of ride towards home.

School him on his own where he feels at ease. At the end of a schooling session is a good time to take him for a short walk on his own, when he is working forwards from your leg aids, he is warmed and settled down. If you find yourself in a tricky situation where he is running back and likely to cause an accident, jump off and lead him forwards. This is not indicative of failure. After all, your aim is to have a horse that you can take with you without the company of another horse. If sometimes he needs to keep you in his sight, it does not matter at all.

The work you are already doing with him sounds absolutely ideal. In time you should be able to build a partnership, with you as the senior partner. Keep telling yourself that it does not matter if achieving perfection takes a long time, as long as both you and the horse are able to enjoy the work and the progress you make. If he suddenly becomes worse or shows signs of finding all his work difficult, then err on the side of caution and have him thoroughly checked over for any physical disabilities.

In the meantime, until he has learnt not to threaten to rear, wear a body protector when you ride, as well as a safe hat. Hopefully, you will never need to put either to the test!

Fliss Gillott

"How high should I fit the bit in my horse's mouth? Does it differ
when fitting a straight bar or a jointed bit?"

Before looking at how bits are fitted it is important to remember that each horse is unique, not only in size and shape of mouth but also in temperament and sensitivity. You will develop a feel for what is right with experience, responding to the way the horse works and the feel he gives you from his mouth. Having said all that, there are a few simple guidelines which one can follow.

The height of the bit in the mouth is taken from its position in the corners of the lips. In other words, viewed without opening the mouth, how much does the bit make the horse 'smile?' With a jointed bit, it is advisable to hold the sides of the bit down from the front, by hooking a finger of each hand over the visible ends of the mouthpiece, before making a final judgement on whether or not the height is correct. When correctly fitted, the bit should just crinkle the corners of the mouth.

If a bit is fitted too low, there is a greater danger of the horse getting his tongue over it. Even without this happening, a low bit will be sloppy and uncomfortable and more likely to cause bruising, especially if it comes into contact with the tushes or premolar teeth. If the cheekpieces bulge when you take up a contact, the bit is too low.

Fitting the bit too high in the mouth will lead to rubbing and pinching at the corners of the mouth. Sometimes this is necessary in the short term to correct a tendency to put the tongue over. In this case, it is kinder not to work for long enough to cause discomfort and certainly not for so long that the bit starts to rub.

Fliss Gillott

When correctly fitted, the bit should just crinkle the corners of the mouth.

How can I calm down my excitable mare at shows?

She is a wonderful TB cross mare who I plan to take to a variety of events over the summer. She gets so excited when I take her anywhere that she is quite unmanageable. As a result I get very tense just knowing that she is likely to 'play up'.

F or any horse which has hitherto led a sheltered life at home, going to a horse show must be a tremendously nerve-wracking experience. Apart from the bustle and tension which probably accompanied the horse at home on the morning of the show, on the journey, and on arrival - new surroundings and strange horses are certain to generate some kind of reaction. For a younger horse, this may be curiosity in the main. For others, this will be tinged with fear and apprehension.

Few people manage to get onto a showground without feeling a level of excitement and show nerves, which is transmitted to the horse and added to his other feelings. All in all, it is not surprising that some horses have great difficulty settling down to their normal levels of good behaviour at a show.

A calm attitude and plenty of preparation will work wonders at a show.

Rider attitude

Your attitude is critical in encouraging your horse to settle. It is difficult to stay calm when your horse is spinning round in circles, refusing to stand still, while you try to unbandage, groom and keep your feet from under hers. However, firm handling and calm good sense will do far more good than shouting.

Do what you have to do as efficiently as possible, expecting the horse to show the same respect for your personal safety as at any other time. In this way, she will be beginning to settle before you start to ride in.

Be prepared!

Make a list of what you will need at the show several days before the show. This gives you time to top up on anything which has run out. Pack the lorry or car in advance, ticking off on your list as you go. Always arrive at the showground in plenty of time to avoid a last minute panic. Have plenty of helpers, but only if they know what they are doing. Nice though it is if Granny turns up with the sandwiches, trying to make small talk often leads to frayed tempers!

Before the show

Work your horse hard the day before a show if she is the type which needs excessive riding in. Although you do not want her to be exhausted, you do want to take the 'edge' off her to reduce stress on the important day.

If you have time before you leave in the morning, work her again then. Allow masses of time before your class, so that you can work her in short bursts rather than grind her down and lose her best performance. Sometimes 10 minutes lungeing followed by a rest, repeated three or four times if necessary, works better than a solid hour's work.

The break gives the horse a chance to gather her thoughts and stop worrying. Some horses always need a long time to settle, but most will start behaving sensibly as they become used to shows being non-stressful occasions.

Perfect timing

Working out how long your horse needs to produce her best performance is only part of the story. How long do you need to produce your best? When do you like to put on your show jacket and shed your chaps?

After working in successfully, a final 10 minutes in full kit, having wiped the bit and cleaned the reins, will give you time to draw breath and relax before the competition. Perhaps a friend has been able to chat to the ring steward and report back with expected class times, so that you can then walk calmly to the ring, looking a million dollars, on your equally calm and gleaming horse.

Fliss Gillott

> ## Nutritional solutions
> See page 28 - the same applies to this problem.
> **Kate Jones**

Could my mare be bored?

She has started to kick her stable door. She is stabled night and day, and gets out for only an hour a day due to lack of time and turnout facilities. Do you think a stable toy would help?

It is obvious that your horse is bored - she has little else to do when confined for the majority of the time. She has also found that kicking stimulates her; it takes energy, makes a noise and she may be doing it because it sometimes hurts. This does not mean that she is a confirmed masochist, but it does mean that she may become one and that the environment in which she is kept needs to be improved.

Horses are social animals. Keeping them in solitary confinement, even if they can see the other horses from time to time, is often just not enough to satisfy their social needs. This is clearly the case with your mare who is showing severe signs of behavioural distress. Thus, the answer is to allow her to have more contact with other horses. Ideally, she needs to be turned out for longer. From what you say, this is not possible at your yard.

You should also look at her feeding. Although she may be getting plenty of food, it may be the wrong type from the behavioural point of view. Horses eat for around 16 hours a day. If she does not have access to food of some type all the time, then what is she going to do with all this time? She will make something to do which may not be what humans desire - like kicking the stable! She should therefore have access to high fibre food 24 hours a day. If you do not want her to eat too much, then make a haynet with very small holes so that she has to work away to get every strand. This will also occupy her time.

Your horse may not be having her cognitive/mental/intellectual needs fulfilled. Horses are very quick learners, and need to live in mentally stimulating environments. Teaching her to do various new things will help her here, and give her something to think about - simple things, like coming when she is called, or shaking hands. You will need to know something about 'learning theory' to do this. For more information, *Horse&Rider* magazine ran a series, which started in April 1999, entitled Equine Education.

Whether or not you have the time for this, it is essential that you make the stable more interesting for her. Stable toys can help for a short while. But the most important point is that you re-think the environment if you want her to give up this behaviour permanently.

Dr Marthe Kiley-Worthington

Main picture: don't let your stable-kept horse become bored or distressed.
Inset: all horses need to live in mentally stimulating environments - you could try teaching yours new activities.

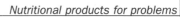

How can I help my horse who is recovering from an injury to the ligaments in his lower leg?

He's 16 years old and has only recently been able to start putting full weight on the leg. Also, how long will it take for him to get back to ridden work?

In horses' legs, the muscles are grouped around the thigh, and around the shoulder, elbow and forearm in the horse. Because of the horse's need to perform at speed, evolution has, over the years, moved all of the musculature to the top of the leg, so that the bottom of the leg is a simple weight bearing strut, moved forward by ligaments.

The superficial and deep flexor tendons, and suspensory ligaments, are the only vital structures around the fetlock joint. In addition to these, the fetlock joint is held together by collateral ligaments, and there is a tendon on the front of the fetlock which is used to pull the leg forward. These tendons and ligaments act as guideropes around the prop.

First aid

First aid treatment for ligament injuries always consists of anti-inflammatory medication, such as the administration of Phenylbutazone by mouth, ice-packing and cold hosing, and the application of open kaolin, between hosing sessions, to draw heat from the limb. This is often combined with light bandaging overnight in an attempt to prevent excessive swelling. However, care has to be taken that the swelling does not continue beneath the bandage and produce pressure-induced skin necrosis (tissue death).

Damage assessment

Having gone through this initial first aid stage, a vet would examine the horse to assess which structures are damaged and how badly they are damaged. The vet may wish to x-ray the area to ensure that the sesamoids have not been injured or to perform an ultrasound scan on the suspensory ligament and flexor tendons.

Finally, some of the pain could be from the fetlock joint capsule itself. This usually manifests itself as heat and swelling in the joint with an obvious fluid 'windgall' between the cannon bone and the suspensory ligament. If your vet is satisfied that there is no other damage, then he may wish to medicate the joint directly by intra-articular injection of drugs to calm down this inflammatory response.

Rob Pilsworth

Nutritional solutions

Ensure the horse has correct nutrients in his diet for repair. Sulphur is the fourth most important element in the body and yet is widely ignored! Sulphur is required for amino acids - the building blocks of soft tissue. Bio-available forms of sulphur, such as methyl sulphonyl methane (MSM) are susceptible to heat and air degradation and therefore lost in preserved and concentrated feed. Supplementation is recommended, with an initial loading dose followed by a low maintenance dose for at least four months. This is the average time taken for full repair, although it is obviously subject to individual variation.

If the x-rays show any cartilage damage - within joints or around the sesamoid bones - the use of chondroprotective agents would also be recommended (see page 14).
Kate Jones

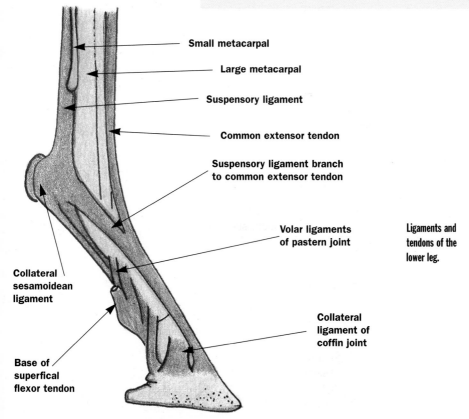

Small metacarpal
Large metacarpal
Suspensory ligament
Common extensor tendon
Suspensory ligament branch to common extensor tendon
Volar ligaments of pastern joint
Collateral sesamoidean ligament
Base of superfical flexor tendon
Collateral ligament of coffin joint

Ligaments and tendons of the lower leg.

"What can I do to help my horse who gets uptight when separated from his friend? He travels with my friend and I, and her horse, to shows and both horses get on extremely well. The problems start when my friend takes her horse away to warm up. My horse gets in a state, leaping about and constantly whinnying. He won't stop until my friend and her horse return.

Horses like to be together. Unless they are taught to realise that they are safe on their own, they will continue to seek the security of other equine companions. There are rare exceptions who will latch onto human company without a backward glance, but they are indeed unusual.

The average horse will continue to cling, and all the more so if it has one single stable mate from which it is hardly ever separated. A horse living on a busy yard, used to the comings and goings of different horses, is less likely to form a strong bond with one particular horse.

The more a horse sees of the world, the more confident he will be in the knowledge that he is not about to be abandoned to the wolves, and that others will come and go without threatening his personal safety. This knowledge does not necessarily help you with a paranoid equine creating havoc in public because it thinks it has been abandoned!

At the show, take the insecure horse away from his friend, rather than the other way round. It is better to be active in a crisis.

Travel alone

Taking a stable companion along for company does not help the situation at all, but rather reinforces the horse's belief that it should not be alone. The only reason for taking a companion is if the horse becomes dangerous to travel without one. Otherwise it is better to make his day out as pleasant as possible with food to eat on the journey, careful driving and firm, yet sympathetic, handling at the event.

Avoid making every trip potentially stressful. Go out on occasions just to meet up with a friend for a quiet hack or a schooling session. Thoroughly condition the horse to being able to cope on his own and eventually he will.

Take the initiative

At a show, take the insecure horse away from his friend rather than the other way round. It is better to be active during a crisis than to be forced into inactivity. Once the horse has been worked in, or is perhaps beginning to feel tired, it is far more likely to settle. Without watching his companion disappear, he will not feel quite so abandoned.

Exhaustion, however, will have the reverse effect. An exhausted horse can feel very vulnerable and actually appear quite the opposite of exhausted whilst it is fighting off its condition. This is more true of hot blooded horses than others.

Keep calm

Avoid losing your temper at all costs. Be firm by all means, but bad temper creates fear and stress which will produce negative results. Never leave the horse unattended if he is obviously getting himself thoroughly upset. This is the time when he is most likely to injure himself, again reinforcing his conviction that he cannot cope alone.

Work alone at home from time to time, eventually out of sight and sound of the horse's regular companions. Insecure horses need constant reassurance, combined with clear leadership, if they are to get hold of themselves and learn to settle.

Fliss Gillott

Nutritional solutions

See page 28 - the same applies to this problem.
Kate Jones

How can I teach my horse to lengthen his strides?

I have recently taken my 12-year-old TB to dressage competitions, and although he is reasonably well schooled, and works in a 'nice' outline, we always have problems when we try to lengthen the stride. What we can do at home to help?

I t is amazing how many riders have a hang-up about lengthening the stride in trot. Lengthening the stride in any of the gaits is dependent on sound, basic schooling, and only goes wrong when the horse is ill-prepared. Couple this with a rider thinking this is an extremely difficult exercise which is best tackled with plenty of gusto, and the end result is the poor horse flying along on his forehand. Sound basic preparation means achieving the following:

● Straightness;
● Impulsion;
● Rhythm.

Straightness

This is not difficult to achieve, but it does require a degree of patience sometimes! See page 18 for advice on this.

Impulsion

Still riding on a straight line, try asking for more impulsion without worrying about lengthening. Does your horse stay straight? Do you stay straight when you use more leg and seat? Ride circles at the beginning and end of your allotted straight line to keep your horse both supple and attentive, remembering to change the rein frequently. Ask for a slower trot or walk whilst maintaining impulsion, and you will find it much easier to maintain those straight lines. Learning to shorten the stride before asking for lengthening will ensure that you have the necessary engagement of the hindlimbs.

Rhythm

There are fringe benefits which come out of this controlled work, including a good rhythm and an improving outline if this has been a problem area. You will find that the horse is working more between leg and hand and that you are beginning to work on every stride he takes. It is like setting the horse up on tramlines, so that when you ask him to go forward with increased impulsion, he stays on those tramlines. Try to keep this feeling when you ride turns and circles, with a strong and regular rhythm, so that these movements encourage the extra flexion of the hindlegs necessary for lengthening.

Equally important is to maintain this straightness through transitions, so that, again, the horse is being prepared for that extra push from behind which is needed in order to lengthen.

Straightness, impulsion and rhythm are all essential prerequisities for lengthened strides.

Ready to lengthen

When you feel the horse is working straight within himself, actively, and in a good rhythm, he is ready to try some lenghtened strides.

Follow these simple steps:

1 Imagine that you are riding up a flight of stairs;
2 Look up and stretch tall;

3 Maintain a contact on both sides of his mouth so that he stays straight and keeps his rhythm;

4 Ask him to move more from your leg.

Softening the inner thigh muscles will help you to sit deep whilst allowing for the extra swing of the horse's back. A few strides at first will be enough before shortening the stride again. As a rider, you will need to get used to the feel of the longer stride, concentrating on keeping yourself off the forehand just as much as the horse. It is important to stay firm but supple around your waist and not to collapse as so many people do when their horse starts to extend. Your horse will need to lift himself higher off the ground in order to go further, and this means lifting through the shoulders. Raising the croup actually pushes the forehand down, and this will happen if you do not make a conscious effort to sit up tall and straight.

Tracking up

Engage a helper on the ground who will, hopefully, be able to tell you when your horse is tracking up, tracking short, or tracking over, if you are not sure of the feel you are getting. In a working trot, the hind foot falls into the print of the front foot. When the stride is lengthened, it goes in front of the front print. This will happen before that spectacular straightening of the forelimb in medium and extended trot.

Although lengthening the stride requires the horse to lengthen his outline to some extent, this need only be slight. Pushing the hands forward to 'allow' the horse to lengthen his neck is more likely to lead to dropping the contact. Following the horse as he lengthens, as long as he stays straight on the bit and in rhythm, is much better. For good lengthening, the feel you should get is relatively slow, powerful and rising up off the ground.

Fliss Gillott

Glossary of nutritional terms

Antioxidant
Naturally sourced antioxidants have the ability to neutralise and remove toxins from the system. Antioxidants are found in many plants but are particularly rich in fruits, dark coloured vegetables (ie spinach, red cabbage) and peppers.

Bio-available
This means the nutrient will be absorbed and is useful to the horse. Many forms of elements, ie elemental sulphur powder, are not bio-available and effectively pass straight through the gut.

Chondroprotective agent
Term given to naturally occurring substances that are beneficial within joints. The two most common are glucosamine and chondroitin sulphate.

Free radical toxin
Small, highly charged, highly damaging toxins released within the system as a result of physiological stress.

Micronutrients
A collective term to describe vitamins, minerals, amino acids and trace elements, that make up a small but vital part of the diet.

Nutraceutical
Taken from 'nutrition' and 'pharmaceutical', it is the term given to a nutrient used for therapy.

Physiological stress
Used to describe any form of stress, not just mental. In the horse this includes any virus, bacterial attack, allergy, infection, traumatic injury, travelling or hard work.

Kate Jones BSc(Hons)
Nutritionist, Natural Animal Feeds

INDEX